Track Athletics

KNOW YOUR SPORT

Clive Gifford

FRANKLIN WATTS
LONDON • SYDNEY

First published in 2006 by
Franklin Watts
338 Euston Road
London NW1 3BH

Franklin Watts Australia
Level 17/207 Kent Street
Sydney NSW 2000

© Franklin Watts 2006
Series editor: Jennifer Schofield
Art director: Jonathan Hair

Series designed and created for Franklin Watts by Painted Fish Ltd.
Designer: Rita Storey
Editor: Nicola Edwards
Photography: Tudor Photography,
    Banbury
Illustrations: Nigel Kitching

A CIP catalogue record
for this book is available
from the British Library.

Dewey classification: 796.42
ISBN 0 7496 64657
Printed in China

Note: At the time of going to press, the statistics and athletes' profiles in this book were up to date. However, due to some athletes' active participation in the sport, it is possible that some of these may now be out of date.

Picture credits
Action plus/Glyn Kirk p.6; Action plus/Mark Cowan/Icon p.7; Action plus/Peter Tarry p.9; Corbis/Bettmann p.13; Action plus/Glyn Kirk p.14; Action plus/Neil Tingle p.21; Action plus/Glyn Kirk p.23 (both); Flora London Marathon p.24; London 2012 p. 26; Action plus/Neil Tingle p.27; Action plus/Glyn Kirk p27.

Cover images: Tudor Photography, Banbury.

All photos posed by models.
Thanks to Jonathan Bean, Hannah Bryan, Jeanette Murrell, Sophie Murrell and Charlie Storey.

The Publisher would like to thank the Banbury Harriers Club and Drayton Athletics Track for using their track.

Taking part in sport is a fun way to get fit, but like any form of physical exercise it has an element of risk, particularly if you are unfit, overweight or suffer from any medical conditions. It is advisable to consult a healthcare professional before beginning any programme of exercise.

Contents

Introduction

Track athletics has millions of fans all over the world. The sport includes a wide range of events – from the explosive 60m and 100m sprints to the ultimate test in endurance, the 42.2-km marathon.

From Ancient to Modern

Since the dawn of history, people have tested their speed against others in races. The first known races were held at Olympia in Ancient Greece almost 2,800 years ago. The ancient Olympic Games were held once every four years until 393CE. Frenchman Baron Pierre de Coubertin founded the modern Olympics in the late 19th century.

The modern Olympics have spurred interest in track athletics enormously. Television broadcasts of the Olympic Games from the 1960s onwards helped boost interest in the top events and athletes. The 2004 Olympics, held in Athens, Greece, were watched by more than one billion viewers.

Major Rewards

At the highest level, elite track athletes are superstars, known the world over. The very top performers are wealthy from prize money, advertising, sponsorship and from appearance fees paid by the organisers of races for them to take part in some events. However, most enter athletics not for the money but for the chance to test themselves against the best runners in the world.

Justin Gatlin wins the 100m final at the 2004 Olympics. Thousands of athletes who may never reach the Olympics still enjoy the thrill of competition and doing their very best. Whatever your ability, there is real pride in recording a personal best (your best ever time in an event) in a race.

ATHENS 2004

Athletics for All

Track athletics is open to people of all ages and abilities. Children and teenagers compete in junior events whilst there are competitions for veteran runners, too. Athletes with disabilities can also take part in a wide range of competitions. The most important are the Paralympics for athletes with physical disabilities and the Special Olympics for people with mental disabilities. Both are held once every four years and attract thousands of competitors and many more spectators.

Germany's Wojtek Czyz wins the 100m at the 2004 Paralympics in 12.51 seconds. Czyz lost his leg after a football accident and runs with a specially designed prosthetic leg. He also won the 200m in a Paralympic world record of 26.18 seconds.

Training for Success

Different events may require different abilities. But all top track athletes train long and hard to build their speed, strength and endurance.

Athlete and Coach

Track athletes train under the supervision of a coach. The coach advises on all parts of an athlete's running technique and builds a training and diet plan for the athlete to follow. A coach may also help an athlete decide what races to run. Many elite athletes stay with the same coach throughout their career.

Power and Speed

Top sprinters need explosive power to run 100m in 10 seconds or less. They build upper-body and leg-muscle strength in the gym but also perform lots of speedwork such as running a series of short sprints. Speedwork helps increase the speed at which their muscles work. Speedwork and some gym training to build strength is also part of longer-distance runners' training.

Increasing Stamina

Middle and long-distance athletes seek to build their stamina levels. Stamina is the ability to work for a long period of time.

Stretching

Here are just a small number of stretches track athletes perform after they have warmed up by jogging and similar exercises. Get your coach to recommend and show you other stretches.

This exercise stretches your calf muscles. Keep the whole of the sole of your rear foot on the floor with the leg extended as you ease forward onto your front foot. Repeat with the other leg. ▶

This exercise stretches the muscles in your thigh called quadriceps. Hold your foot up to your bottom keeping a straight back for a count of ten then repeat with your other leg. You can use your spare arm for balance. ▶

Some long-distance runners, such as marathon world record-holder Paula Radcliffe, train by running as many as 220 kilometres a week.

Stretching a Point

All track athletes warm up and stretch before training or racing. A thorough warm-up and stretch helps prevent injuries such as muscle tears and strains. It also gets the body's muscles working at their peak.

Track Spikes

Track athletes often train in training shoes, but in competition they wear spiked shoes. These feature a pattern of short, sharp spikes on the ball of the sole. The spikes help provide grip on the track without slowing the athlete down. Sprinters wear the lightest weight spiked shoes of all. Some of these shoes weigh as little as 120 grams.

Carl Lewis

Date of birth: July 1st, 1961

Nationality: American

Track records

Gold – Olympics 100m (1984, 1988), 200m (1984), 4x100m relay (1984, 1992), World Championships 100m (1983, 1987, 1991), 4x100m relay (1983, 1987, 1991)

Silver – World Championships 200m (1988)

As a young boy, Frederick Carlton 'Carl' Lewis did not have an athlete's physique and was bullied. But meeting the Olympic legend, Jesse Owens (see page13), inspired him to train long and hard. The results were spectacular. Lewis won four gold medals at the 1984 Olympics and over his career totalled five Olympic track golds as well as a further four in the long jump.

To perform this hamstring stretch, sit on the floor with your knees straight and reach to touch and hold your toes. Hold the position with the back of your knees and legs in contact with the ground before releasing.

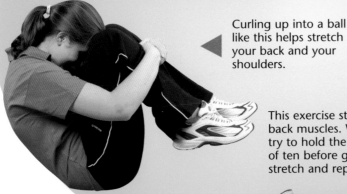

Curling up into a ball like this helps stretch your back and your shoulders.

This exercise stretches your lower back muscles. With all stretches, try to hold the position for a count of ten before gently releasing the stretch and repeating.

In Competition

Athletes need to train hard to develop their fitness and their running technique to prepare for competition, whether it is a school race or an Olympic final.

On Track

Apart from the marathon and race walking, all events take place on the track. In the past, tracks were just grass or hard ground. The surfaces of today's athletics tracks are carefully engineered to provide grip without slowing the athletes down. In 200m, 400m and 800m races, the start positions are staggered. This is so that athletes all have the same distance to run to the finish line.

Starting Blocks

When US sprinter Jesse Owens won his four gold medals at the 1936 Olympics, he had no starting blocks, just small holes dug in the cinder track. Today, nearly all sprinters have starting blocks which can be adjusted for different leg lengths.

Wind Speed

The wind speed is measured and displayed at the trackside at major competitions. A wind which blows behind runners (called a tailwind) helps runners. If a tailwind is over 2 metres per second, then any records set in the race are not officially recognised, but the result of the race still stands.

A standard outdoor athletics track is 400m in length with two bends and two straights. The track features markings for different race events.

▼

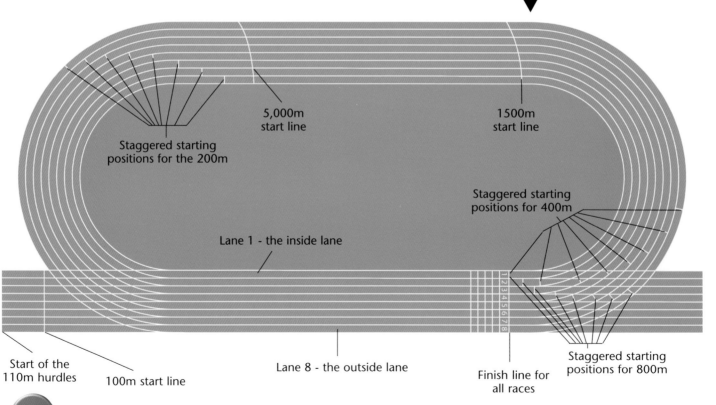

Staggered starting positions for the 200m

5,000m start line

1500m start line

Staggered starting positions for 400m

Lane 1 - the inside lane

Lane 8 - the outside lane

Staggered starting positions for 800m

Start of the 110m hurdles

100m start line

Finish line for all races

In many races, runners must stay in their own lane for part or all of the race. If they stray into another lane (as above), they will be disqualified.

In competition, track athletes are given their own race number which they must wear on their clothing. Track athletes usually wear close-fitting all-in-one suits or lightweight running vests tucked into high-cut shorts.

One of Many

Track athletes must run a number of races before reaching the final of a major competition. Top athletes may have to run trials races in their own country. The best performers in these trials are often the athletes who will go on to represent their country. At the competition, athletes may have to take part in rounds of qualifying races, called heats. The best runners progress into the later rounds and, eventually, the final.

Drug-testing

A large number of drugs are banned from sport. Some are prohibited because they can improve performance and give an unfair advantage. Many drugs are harmful to athletes' health. Today, top athletes are regularly tested to find out if any of these illegal drugs are in their bodies, usually through taking a sample of their urine. Athletes may be tested before, during or after a major competition. Athletes found to have taken a prohibited substance may be banned from competing in the sport.

The Sprints 1

The fastest athletes in the world compete in the sprint events. Outdoors, these are the 100m, 200m and 400m. Indoors, the 100m is replaced by the 60m sprint. Elite sprinters reach incredible speeds – up to about 40km/hour.

Starter's Orders

The starter is in charge of sprint races. At major races, the starter uses a special gun linked to the electronic timer. Sprint races begin with a series of three commands from the starter. The final command is "Go!" or the firing of the starting gun.

The Sprint Start

1 *On the starter's order of "On your marks", the sprinter gets into her starting blocks. Her arms are straight but not locked at the elbow. Her hands are placed slightly more than shoulder-width apart.*

Shoulders are back and above or slightly ahead of hands.

2 *On the order of "Set", the sprinter gets into her starting position with her hips higher than her shoulders. Her feet are pushed hard back into the blocks. The athlete focuses down the track.*

False Starts

If a sprinter leaves the starting blocks before the start gun is fired, it is a false start. Only one false start in a race is allowed. The second person to have a false start is automatically disqualified from the race.

At championships, false starts are detected by electronic sensors in the athletes' starting blocks. The sensors are linked to a computer and the starter's gun.

Jesse Owens

Date of birth: September 12th, 1913 (died: 1980)

Nationality: American

Events: 100m, 200m, 400m, 4x100m relay, 4x400m relay, long jump

Height: 1.78m

Weight: 75kg

Gold: Olympics 100m, 200m, 4x400m relay, long jump (1936)

Born to a poor family, James Cleveland Owens turned to athletics at the age of eight. Attending Ohio State University, he competed in 42 track events in his junior year, winning them all. In 1935, he broke a clutch of world records in a single afternoon at a Big Ten athletics meeting. The following year at the Berlin Olympics, Owens amazed spectators with gold medals in the 100m, the 200m, the 4x400m relay and the long jump.

Arm on rear leg side is thrown back.

3 As the starting gun fires, the sprinter's hands leave the ground. Her front leg drives hard against the block. The rear leg comes through as quickly as possible to take the first forward stride.

Arms pass close to body's sides. Shoulders are down.

Rear leg drives through.

4 For the next 20m-30m, the sprinter drives herself forward. She keeps her body and head low. Her arms pump back and forth, not across her body. Her hands are relaxed with her fingers not tensed into a fist.

Head and body point straight down middle of the lane. Head and body are kept as still as possible.

5 The sprinter's body gradually straightens up as she reaches top speed. Her front leg drives forward with a high knee action. At its highest point, the thigh should be parallel with the ground. Her rear leg is fully extended as it pushes off the track.

13

The Sprints 2

A great start is essential for sprinting success, but just as important is a powerful running style. Sprint athletes aim to maintain a relaxed body position right up to and through the finishing line.

Keeping the Speed

Once they reach top speed, sprinters aim to maintain it all the way to the finish line. In the last stages of a sprint race, the body suffers fatigue from all the effort. It is then that the sprinters really concentrate on keeping their body relaxed. If they tense their arms, legs and shoulders, they will lose a lot of speed.

Running the Bend

In races longer than 100m, runners have to run on the bend of the track. Running at top speed pushes the sprinter to the outside edge of their lane. Runners must take care not to step outside their lane or they will be disqualified.

Fast Finish

A runner finishes a race when their upper body crosses the finish line.

▶ Running a 200m bend, the French athlete Marie-Jose Perec drops her inside arm a little and leans slightly into the bend. She aims to run towards the inside of her lane which is the shortest route to the finish line.

Arms, legs and head do not count. Some runners perform a dip to push their upper body forward as they approach the finish line, but poor timing of the dip can lose vital places and time.

Photo Finishes

At top competitions, high-speed photos are taken of the finish. These are used to separate positions in particularly close races. At the 1993 World Championships in Stuttgart, Germany, Merlene Ottey and Gail Devers both recorded exactly the same time, 10.82 seconds, in the 100m final. However, the photo finish made Ottey the winner, just.

Track Fact

In the 1940s, many male athletics coaches thought female athletes with children should not compete in case they injured themselves. Dutch mother-of-two Fanny Blankers-Koen proved them wrong by winning four gold medals at the 1948 Olympics. In her career she broke 16 world records.

Fast Finish

1. *The sprinter is upright and running smoothly with his hands and shoulders relaxed as he heads towards the finish line. His head and eyes are pointing straight ahead.*

2. *The sprinter times his dip, thrusting his chest forwards and his arms back. He aims to run through the line at top speed.*

Relay Racing

There are two relay races for men and women – the 4x100m and the 4x400m. Both races involve teams of four sprinters, each completing a leg of the race while holding a 28-30cm-long baton, which they must pass to their team-mates.

4x400m Relay

The first runner runs in a lane as in the 400m sprint. At the changeover, the first runner passes the baton to the second runner, who starts in their lane but after 100m can move to the inside lane. The baton changeover to the third and fourth

Track Fact

At the 2005 World Athletics Championships, the US team were red-hot favourites as they included world 100m and 200m champion Justin Gatlin. In a heat, they dropped the baton and were out of the race.

4x100m Changeover

1 *As the passer approaches, the receiver starts to sprint forward. Her receiving arm trails back but her body faces the front.*

Receiver's palm faces upwards.

2 *As the receiver builds up speed, the incoming runner must judge when the baton can be passed and often shouts a signal. She sweeps the baton downwards into the receiver's hand.*

runners occurs on the finish line of each lap with those waiting for the baton looking to get in the best position. The fourth runner in a 4x400m event is often the team's fastest sprinter.

In the Zone

Passing the baton on in the 4x100m must take place in a 20-m stretch called the changeover zone. A 10-m stretch of track lies before the changeover zone. Called the acceleration zone, it allows receivers to run to build up speed before the baton changeover. The baton exchange must take place completely in the changeover zone or the team is disqualified.

4x100m Changeover

The changeover is where many relay races are won or lost. Athletes practise the changeover so that it is as smooth and error-free as possible. The incoming runner tries to maintain their speed as much as possible.

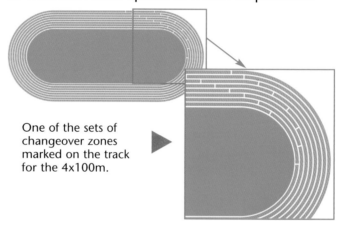

One of the sets of changeover zones marked on the track for the 4x100m.

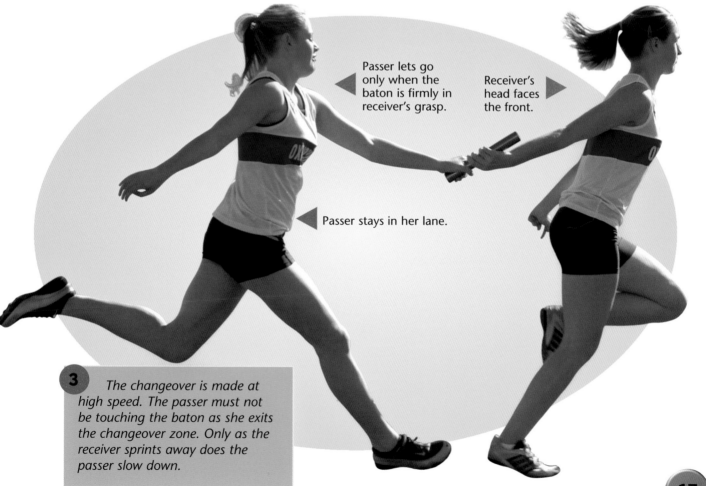

Passer lets go only when the baton is firmly in receiver's grasp.

Receiver's head faces the front.

Passer stays in her lane.

3 *The changeover is made at high speed. The passer must not be touching the baton as she exits the changeover zone. Only as the receiver sprints away does the passer slow down.*

Hurdles

The hurdles are fast-paced track events. In these races, athletes have to sprint and clear ten hurdles which are spaced at regular intervals in their track lane before reaching the finish line.

Different Races

The sprint hurdles are held over 110m for men and 100m for women. The 400m hurdles for men and women features slightly lower hurdles but is an extremely tiring race. Athletes have to fight against their fatigue to keep going over the final few hurdles.

Sprint Hurdling

Opposite arm to front leg drives forwards for balance.

Arm on the front leg side is thrown back.

Foot is turned outwards to clear hurdle.

2 *The front leg is thrown over the hurdle with the arm on the opposite side of the body also thrown forward for balance. The rear leg is pulled up at the knee.*

1 *Approaching the hurdle, the athlete uses her rear leg to drive herself up and forward. Her front leg bends high and lifts into the air.*

Stride Pattern

A body moves slower whilst in the air than on the ground. The aim of good hurdling is to reduce the time spent clearing the hurdle and to get back on the track as quickly as possible. Athletes plan how many strides they take between hurdles so that they get a good rhythm in their hurdling. This is called their stride pattern.

Knocked Over

The hurdles have a wooden top on a tubular metal frame and are designed to topple over easily if knocked, but only from the right direction. Never try to clear the hurdle from the wrong side as you may injure yourself.

Sprint Hurdling

Hurdlers work really hard on their hurdling technique in training so that it becomes a smooth, flowing series of movements.

3 As the hurdle is cleared, the heel of the rear leg is brought up to the bottom. The front leg is brought back down onto the track as quickly as possible.

Rear foot is pulled through and lands ahead.

4 As the athlete lands on their front foot, the rear leg is pulled forward and ahead of the hurdler. The athlete sprints away, staying upright.

Track Fact

At the very first modern Olympics in 1896, the 100m hurdles race featured heavy sheep barriers as hurdles. These were nailed into place on the track and could cause injury if they were hit hard by an athlete.

19

Middle-distance Running

Middle-distance running's two main events are the 800m and 1500m. They are amongst the most exciting races because they combine raw speed with strength and tactics.

Starting Positions
In the 800m, the runners line up in staggered starting positions. Each athlete is in their own lane, just like in the sprints, and must not leave that lane for the first 100m of the race. In the 1500m, athletes line up in any place they choose on the curved starting line. As soon as the race begins, they can break for the inside lane.

Standing Start
Runners often use a standing start for middle-distance running. The runners get two calls from the starter, "On your marks" and "Go!". When the first command is made, they stand with their front foot just behind the start line in a low position with knees bent. As the race begins, they drive hard off their front foot and move away.

Running Style
Middle-distance runners run on the balls of their feet with an upright body position. Their arms swing back and forth to help generate forward movement.

The Last Lap
In middle-distance and long-distance events, a bell is rung trackside as the athletes begin the last lap. Runners try to get in a good position and it is here that a runner's strength and speed really count. The best runners will still have plenty of energy in reserve for a powerful sprint finish.

Standing Start

The athlete is poised to start with his weight on his front foot.

Track Fact
Kenyan athlete Kip Keino was caught in a traffic jam shortly before the 1500m Olympic final in 1968. He had to jog 2km to the stadium but went on, minutes later, to win the race.

Rounding the Bend

1 *Running on the last bend, the second-placed runner does not want to get trapped by the runner in front and by other athletes coming up on her outside. This is called being boxed in.*

2 *The second athlete increases her speed and moves out of the inside lane so that she is on the shoulder of the lead runner. She must be careful to avoid a clash of legs with other runners.*

3 *With an extra kick, the athlete overtakes the lead runner and keeps driving forward.*

Kelly Holmes

Nationality: British

Date of birth: April 19th, 1970

Event: 800m, 1500m

Height: 1.64m

Weight: 55kg

Gold - Commonwealth Games 1500m (1994, 2002), Olympics 800m,1500m (2004)

Silver – World Championships 1500m (1995), 800m (2003), World Indoor 1500m (2003)

Bronze – World Championships 800m (1995), European Championships 800m (2002)

After winning English schools' titles, Kelly Holmes joined the army and became a physical training instructor. She did not turn to full-time athletics until 1997. Holmes suffered a number of injuries, often just before major championships, but refused to be beaten. At the age of 34, she amazed spectators at the 2004 Olympics by running from the back of the pack and relying on her strength to win both the 800m and 1500m.

Long-distance Running

The 3,000m steeplechase, the 5,000m and the 10,000m are the best-known long-distance track events. They place enormous demands on runners' bodies. Elite runners take just over a minute to complete each lap of the race. And they still need pace in reserve for a sprint finish to the line.

Running Style

Long-distance runners must not waste energy, so they train hard on making their running technique as smooth, relaxed and efficient as possible.

Laps

The 10,000m involves 25 laps of a 400m track. A lap indicator board is positioned near the finish line. It shows how many laps remain.

Pacing the Race

Long-distance runners aim to run at an even speed throughout much of the race to conserve energy. Some runners prefer to lead a race from the front, but it is hard work. The front runner encounters more air resistance so you will often see runners taking turns to lead the field with other athletes tucked in behind.

Long-distance Running Style

1 The runner's head and body is upright and relaxed with the shoulders low. As the runner pushes off his rear leg, he extends it behind him.

2 The front leg is lifted with a high knee action. This is called the pick up. The arms swing back and forth close beside the body.

Steeplechase

The 3,000m steeplechase features sturdy wooden barriers, 91.4cm high for men and 76.2cm high for women, which cannot be knocked over like hurdles, and a water jump which includes a 3.66m-long pit of water. The steeplechasers have to hurdle 28 barriers and cross seven water jumps in a race.

Clearing the Water Jump

Steeplechasers may hurdle the regular barriers but use a different technique to clear the water jump. They place the front foot on the top of the barrier and, keeping their body low, drive off it. They aim to land in the shallower water at the far end of the jump.

3 *The front leg extends and hits the ground. As the front leg lands, the rear leg swings through. The athlete runs on the balls of his feet.*

Haile Gebrselassie

Nationality: Ethiopian

Date of Birth: April 19th, 1973

Event: 5,000m, 10,000m

Height: 1.65m

Weight: 54kg

Gold – Olympics 10,000m (1996, 2000), World Championships 10,000m (1993, 1995, 1997, 1999), World Indoor 3,000m (1997, 1999)

Silver – World Championships 5,000m (1993)

Growing up on an isolated farm, Gebrselassie used to run 10km to school every day. He made an immediate impact on the competitive scene winning both the 5,000m and 10,000m at the 1994 World Junior Championships. Often running from the front, the incredibly popular Ethiopian was the first to break 13 minutes for the 5,000m and 27 minutes for the 10,000m.

Marathon and Race Walking

The marathon is the ultimate in long-distance running – just over 42km of gruelling racing faces each marathon runner. The ultimate in race walking competitions is even longer, with race walkers taking on a 50-km race.

Different Courses

Each marathon course is different and top runners usually check the course and plan their run in advance. Most of the race takes place on public roads, though at major championships the race finishes in the stadium.

Race Tactics

Some marathon runners like to lead from the front to force a fast pace and to tire their opponents. Others seek to stay in the leading group and gradually wind up the pace in the later stages or strike with a surge at a certain point. Whatever their tactics, runners take great note of the climate and conditions and drink lots of fluids at regular intervals.

Marathons for All

It is not only the world's elite runners who take part in marathons. City marathons held all over the world feature thousands of amateur runners who train hard and often raise large sums of money for charities. The Berlin, London and New York marathons are giants, each with over 30,000 finishers every year.

Thousands of runners crowd the streets in the annual London Marathon.

1 *The race walker moves with an upright stance and his arms swinging across his chest. He keeps a straight right leg with firm contact on the ground as he brings his rear leg through.*

2 *His left leg lands heel-first on the track followed smoothly by a movement onto the ball of his foot. Only when his left leg has made solid contact with the ground, does he bring his right leg through to take another stride.*

Race Walking

Race walking is a long-distance event over 10km, 20km and 50km, with shorter events for amateur athletes. The event features a special walking technique. A part of one foot must always be in contact with the ground with a straight leg. Officials watch the athletes carefully and breaking the rules can lead to disqualification from the race.

Race walkers need to have incredible control of their body. Good technique sees the athlete walking with both feet landing on an imaginary straight line ahead. Movement from the walker's hips generates a distinctive wiggle and it also helps to lengthen the walker's stride so that each step covers a slightly greater distance than ordinary walking.

Track Fact
Champion race walkers complete a 20-km race in only 15-25 minutes more time than it takes runners to cover the same distance.

The Big Competitions

Top track athletes get the chance to test themselves against the very best at a series of major competitions held all over the world. Here are some of the biggest competitions of them all.

The Olympic Games

Since their start in 1896, the modern Olympics have grown to become the biggest sports event on earth. Held every four years, track athletics is the jewel in the crown and winning an Olympic gold medal on the track makes an athlete world famous. There have been some extraordinary Olympic winners on the track including the outstanding runner, Paavo Nurmi. This Finnish athlete dominated long-distance running in the 1920s, winning nine gold and three silver medals in three Olympic Games.

World Athletics Championships

Second only to the Olympics, the World Athletics championships have been held since 1983 and now take place every two years. They are always held in a different year to the Olympics. At the 2005 championships in Helsinki, Finland, the 3,000m steeplechase for women was introduced for the first time.

The 2008 Olympics will be held in Beijing, China, and the 2012 Games will be hosted by London. This is an artist's impression of the 2012 athletics stadium which is being built in east London.

Lacena Golding-Clarke, wearing the yellow colours of Jamaica, battles for the lead in the semi-final of the women's 60m hurdles at the 2003 World Indoor Championships in Birmingham, England.

The Commonwealth Games

First held in 1930 as a competition for territories of the British Empire, the Commonwealth Games now attracts athletes from over 70 nations. The four countries of the United Kingdom – England, Scotland, Wales and Northern Ireland – all compete separately. The 2002 Games in Manchester, England, drew huge crowds with athletes such as Jana Pittman, of Australia, winning the 400m hurdles, England's Paula Radcliffe the 5,000m and Namibian Frankie Fredericks winning the 200m.

World Indoor Championships

Indoor track athletics takes place on a 200m-long track which has banked bends to aid fast running. The 100m and 110m hurdles are replaced by 60m versions and the longest race run on the indoor track tends to be the 3,000m. Held approximately every two years since 1985, the World Indoor Championships are the biggest indoor track athletics competition of all.

Australian athlete Cathy Freeman runs the second leg of the 4x400m at the 2002 Commonwealth Games.

Selected World Records

100m Records

Men

100m 9.77sec Asafa Powell (Jamaica)
14 June 2005

Women

100m 10.49sec Florence Griffith-Joyner (USA)
16 July 1988

Long-distance Records

Men

5,000m 12min:37.35sec Kenenisa Bekele (Ethiopia)
31 May 2004

10,000m 26min:17.53sec Kenenisa Bekele (Ethiopia)
26 August 2005

Women

5,000m 14min:24.68sec Elvan Abeylegesse (Turkey)
11 June 2004

10,000m 29min:31.78sec Wang Junxia (China)
8 September 1993

Longest-standing Major Track World Record

800m 1min:53.28sec Jarmila Kratochvílová
(Czechoslovakia) 26 July 1983

Marathon Records

Men 2hrs:04min:55sec Paul Tergat (Kenya)
28 September 2003

Women 2hrs:15min:25sec Paula Radcliffe (Great
Britain) 13 April 2003

Relay Records

Men

4x100m Relay 37.40sec USA
8 August 1992

4x400m Relay 2min:54.20sec USA
22 July 1998

Women

4x100m Relay 41.37sec East Germany
6 October 1985

4x400m Relay 3min:15.17sec Soviet Union
1 October 1988

Middle-distance Records

Men

800m 1min:41.11sec Wilson Kipketer (Denmark)
24 August 1997

1,500m 3min:26.00sec Hicham El Guerrouj (Morocco)
14 July 1998

Women

1500m 3min:50.46sec Qu Yunxia (China)
11 Sep 1993

800m 1min:53.28sec Jarmila Kratochvílová
(Czechoslovakia) 26 July 1983

200m and 400m

Men

200m 19.32sec Michael Johnson (USA)
1 August 1996

400m 43.18sec Michael Johnson (USA)
26 August 1999

Women

200m 21.34sec Florence Griffith Joyner (USA)
29 September 1988

400m 47.60sec Marita Koch (East Germany)
6 October 1985

Hurdles Records

Men

110m Hurdles 12.91sec held jointly by Colin Jackson (Great
Britain) 20 August 1993 and Xiang Liu (China) 27 August
2004

400m Hurdles 46.78sec Kevin Young (USA)
6 August 1992

Women

100m Hurdles 12.21sec Yordanka Donkova (Bulgaria)
20 August 1988

400m Hurdles 52.34sec Yuliya Pechonkina (Russia)
8 August 2003

First Person to Break the Four-minute Mile

Roger Bannister (England)
May 1954

Glossary

Baton The short tube passed between relay runners.

Break To build a gap between a runner or small group of middle- or long-distance runners and the rest of the pack.

Changeover zone The part of the track where the baton must be exchanged in a relay race.

Dip finish Finishing a track race by forcing the chest ahead of the rest of the body.

Disqualification To be thrown out of an event. If the race has been run, to lose your position.

Elite Top, usually professional, athletes.

Fatigue Tiredness after performing an activity.

Heat A qualifying race in an event with the best finishers advancing to the next round of the competition.

Pack The main group of runners in a middle- or long-distance race.

Personal best Your best ever time for a particular event, sometimes referred to as a PB.

Physique The shape of an athlete's body.

Split times The times an athlete achieves for different parts of a race.

Staggered start Starting blocks arranged so that each athlete runs exactly the same distance whatever lane they are drawn in.

Websites

www.olympic.org
The home page of the International Olympic Committee and full of features and profiles of top sprinters and other track athletes.

www.iaaf.org
The website of the IAAF, the organization that runs world athletics.

www.wada-ama.org
The home on the Internet of the World Anti-Doping Agency (WADA). The website has many features and news stories on drug-testing and banned substances.

www.ukathletics.net
The UK Athletics website with lots of information on UK records, profiles of elite athletes, details of athletics clubs and how to get involved in the sport.

www.athletics.org.au
Athletics Australia's website is packed with track athletes' biographies as well as news and features and a section aimed at secondary school students.

Note to parents and teachers: every effort has been made by the Publishers to ensure that these websites are suitable for children, that they are of the highest educational value, and that they contain no inappropriate or offensive material. However, because of the nature of the Internet, it is impossible to guarantee that the contents of these sites will not be altered. We strongly advise that Internet access is supervised by a responsible adult.

Index